No Guns Left Behind:
Poems
about Mass Shootings
on US School Campuses

Mickey J. Corrigan

Dedicated to all the people
who have lost their lives in senseless school shootings
in the US.
And to the kids from Parkland
who are doing something about it.

Contents

Note from the Author

The school shootings depicted in the following poems are only a partial listing of the many school massacres committed in the US. The list is not comprehensive and therefore leaves out hundreds of instances of gun violence on American school campuses. In each of the poems, the gunman remains unnamed to avoid additional attention and antihero status. In each of the atrocities described, multiple people were killed or many were wounded—or both.

In situations like these, really, there are no words. But sometimes you have to find them.

Acknowledgments

Much gratitude for the hearts and eyes of Brenda Ferber and Debbie Fischer, who provided essential feedback on all of these poems.

Some of these poems have appeared in literary journals including:

Fourth & Sycamore: "Dance Dance Revolution," "13 Minutes," "Future Mass Shooter," "Hurt in 42," "School Strong"

Down in the Dirt: "Allure of the Disaffected," "The Evidence," "Red Lake," "The Question Mark Kid," "This is Not a Whodunit"

Adelaide Magazine: "13 Seconds"

Poets Reading the News: "Post-Parkland"

Enoch Brown and Night Walker, 1764

It was a matter of lives
of the children said the braves
before tomahawks rained down
on scalp after small sweet scalp
hair washed by mothers in torn dresses
out by the creek, fat babies
on ribby backs
and the teacher stood tall
in worn slippers, hair long
beard full, he said
not the children.

But it was a matter of honor
the politics of children, lives
of others said the braves
and gunshot hit the mark
and he fell to the dirt floor
nine children dying
the first school shooting
when life was hard
and children died all the time
parents weeping and failing
as we do now.

But it was a matter of violation
of policy and the old Indians
branded those braves
cowards,
Night Walker the old chief
turned his ribby back. Too late
the young men stained
with the blood of babies
and unknowingness.

That stain lingers
to this day
on young men's hands.

*Pontiac's War in 1764 included a massacre at a Pennsylvania school
house in which teacher Enoch Brown and nine students were killed
by four young American Indians. Afterward, the Lenape braves were
ostracized by their old chief, Night Walker, for their cowardice.*

Texas Tower

You set your sites on
the highest point in town
with a maximum range
and full inaccessibility
for the enemy below.

Who is the enemy now
you wonder as you drive
to the university and rise
to the tower top
your footlocker full of guns
700 rounds of ammunition
the tumor in your head
the size of a full metal jacket.

Who is the enemy now
you lock and load
you, the sharpshooter
in the Marines, top gun
at home
at a loss
the wife you killed
and left behind

and the marksman in you
takes over, perfect aim
from the deck of the tower
aim true, hand steady, you site
the enemy

who is the enemy

you shoot to kill
you shoot to kill
you shoot to kill
you shoot to kill
you shoot to kill you shoot to kill you shoot to kill you shoot to kill
you shoot to kill you shoot to kill you shoot to kill you shoot to kill
you shoot to kill you shoot to kill
the enemy

you, who
shoots to kill.

In one of the deadliest school shootings in US history, a 25-year-old veteran transported a cache of weapons in a footlocker to the University of Texas at Austin on August 1, 1966. From the observation tower in the main building, the former Marine shot random people on campus, killing 14 and injuring 31. On autopsy, a tumor was found in his brain, which some experts say may explain his violent outburst.

13 Seconds

And bombs dropping overseas
where the war continues killing
the people and young soldiers
lose time, limbs, their minds
and the heroin's cheap
on campuses the students
in torn jeans smoke weed
talk revolution, form lines
around buildings, chained
to the ivy-covered walls
and the bombs drop
in Cambodia and students
at Kent State and everywhere
stand up and march, chanting
to the universal gods
peace in our time
and the National Guard
Ohio's young soldiers
lose their minds
destroying lives
like other shattered soldiers
at VAs across the country
killing
four students
wounding
nine people
sixty-seven rounds
in thirteen seconds

no peace in our time.

On May 4, 1970, unarmed college students were gunned down by 28 members of the Ohio National Guard. Some of the students were participating in a protest against the bombing of Cambodia by the US military, others were merely walking across campus. Four were killed, 9 others injured. In response to the unjustified violence, hundreds of American schools closed as more than 4 million students went on strike. The tragedy was memorialized in the popular protest song by Crosby, Stills, Nash and Young, "Ohio."

Evergreen

On the rolling campus
seven pines stand tall
roses bloom, students study
quiet in the cool hush
of the university library

where the ex-Marine
thought his fellow employees
watched porno films

starring his wife!
a secret porn star!

And he stood tall
fought back, brought
a semiautomatic rifle
to work and hunted
all the dirty voyeurs
down.

Soldiers stand tall
with honor
find their way
he found his way
to the library
he cleaned each day
he cleaned it up
removing stains
sick laughter, sidelong glances
he fought with honor
for his wife.

Under seven evergreens
old memories stand tall
in clean green air
two custodians, a graphic artist
grad student, professor
a photographer,
son of the dean.

*On July 12, 1976, a delusional custodian brought a rifle to the
university library where he worked. The ex-Marine roamed the lobby
and media center, killing 7 and injuring 2, most fellow employees
whom he believed to be screening porn starring his estranged wife.
He called the police to turn himself in, stating, "I went berserk at Cal
State Fullerton and I committed a terrible act." He was diagnosed
with paranoid schizophrenia and institutionalized in the state of
California.*

Mondays

She's sixteen
five-two, bright
red hair in the window
barricaded
inside her house, single
mattress on the floor
shared with Dad.

I don't like Mondays
she says
aims out the window
at the school across the street
a BB gun, then
a semiautomatic rifle
aimed at little kids.

I don't like Mondays.
This livens it up
she says and
the principal dies
saving the children
the custodian dies
saving the children
a policeman lies bleeding
eight children on the ground.

I asked for a radio
and he gave me a gun
she says later
blames her father
the whiskey and beer bottles
scattered around the house

her epilepsy
her bike injury
that single mattress
on the dirty floor.

I don't like Mondays
shoots out the windows
shoots up the children
shoots down her future

spends Mondays
in jail.

On January 29, 1979, a 16-year-old girl shot 10 people from the window of her house in San Diego. The children were lined up at the gate to the Cleveland Elementary School, waiting to begin the day. Later, Bob Geldorf and the Boomtown Rats wrote the song "I Don't Like Mondays," which became a top hit in the UK. In 1989, another shooting occurred at another Cleveland Elementary School, this one in Stockton, California, with 5 killed and 30 wounded.

Zero Equals Infinity

When he pulls up in the van
he can smell the pines
fresh needles in spring sunlight
and the gasoline bomb
in the back seat.

His manifesto says:
Threaten one and all are at your mercy!

His crew has bailed
they refuse to help
create a brave new world
full of brilliant children
like Cokeville Elementary.

This is a revolution!

His loyal wife lures them
down the Pine-Sol hall
a job applicant, the UPS man, teachers
and children, laughing children
following like baby ducks
to the first grade classroom
finger paintings on the walls
little toadstool desks.

Zero equals infinity.

He corrals the hostages
with the bomb
in the classroom
where the children

sob and curl up
watch TV, read stories
sing happy birthday and pray
to the women in white
floating overhead.

Two million per child and an audience with the president!

He ties the shoelace
to his loyal wife's wrist
the touchy trigger
but she twitches…
smoke and fire fill the room
so he shoots her
then himself
the children screaming

the angels urging them out
the open window
to the sweet smelling arms
of the thick green forest.

On May 16, 1986, a former policeman fired for misconduct arrived at the Cokeville Elementary School in Cokeville, Wyoming. He and his wife held 136 children and 18 adults hostage with guns and a gasoline bomb. When the bomb accidentally exploded, the man shot his wife and killed himself. His manifesto stated his plan to start a brave new world with intelligent children. Some of the children claimed angels in white floated overhead, urging them to go to the window to avoid getting hurt. Although 76 were wounded, all of the hostages survived.

Does Not Fit
"This is a case where the punishment does not fit the crime."
—Judge Ralph Wilson after sentencing two shooters aged 11 and 13

His mother married an inmate.
                  His father gave him a gun
                    when he turned 6.
Two middle school boys
played alone
in the woods of Arkansas
met on the school bus
joined forces
made mad plans.

His grandfather had a wildlife job,
unlocked guns.
                  His mother had a van.
Soon they had 9 guns
2000 rounds
and a getaway car.

He pulled the fire alarm.
                   He hid in the bushes.
Their classmates filed out
both took aim, fired
                    fired, fired, fired, fired...

State found them both guilty
but mandated release
on their 21st birthdays.

The only two school shooters
in a country of school shooters
not dead

not incarcerated
not punished enough.

It's never enough.

On March 24, 1998, two boys hid a cache of stolen guns in the bushes by their middle school outside Jonesboro, Arkansas. After setting off the fire alarm, they shot at their fellow students, killing 4 as well as a teacher, injuring 10 others. Arrested as they fled the scene, the boys were tried as juveniles in a state where the law did not allow young people to be tried as adults. Since their release from detention, one has been arrested with a gun, the other has filed for a concealed carry permit.

The Evidence

Consider the gun
stolen
by a friend
from a friend's dad
in the brown paper bag
in the dented locker
at school.

Consider the expulsion,
the suspension
a droplet in a dark pool
unseen, spreading
humiliation
ridicule, threats
of military school.

Consider the boy's bedroom
a new rifle
a Glock pistol
ammo in another room
shooting lessons
visits to psychiatrists,
special education, help.

Consider the good parents
considerate parents
on the bathroom floor
gaping holes in the back
of their middle-aged heads.

Consider the trench coat
the knives and loaded weapons

1127 rounds
up and down hallways
the shots and screams
blood splattering tile.

Watch a fellow student
shot in the chest
tackle the shooter,
pinning him down
until help arrives.

I want to consider
that boy,
his lung collapsed
his young arms pressed
against the killer's throat.

*A 15-year-old student was suspended from Thurston High School in
Springfield, Oregon, for having a loaded weapon in his locker. On
May 21, 1998, he shot and killed his parents before returning to
school armed with two pistols, a rifle, and hunting knives. He
roamed the grounds, killing 2 students and wounding 25. While he
reloaded, a wounded student tackled him, then 6 others piled on,
holding the shooter until help arrived. He is now serving a 111-year
prison sentence.*

Allure of the Disaffected

The terror plot:
start a distraction fire
blow up the cafeteria
blow up the parking lot
blow up the school
shoot the survivors
become famous
BECOME FAMOUS
in video
on TV
online
infamous
antiheroes
hijack a plane
fly it into a building
die as martyrs
to an unjust system:
high school.

It doesn't matter now.

Black duffle bags
with pipe bombs, car bombs
explosive devices
Molotov cocktails
sawed off shotguns
ammo from Kmart
they arrive on campus.

I like you now.
Get out of here, go home.

In caps and trench coats
of fear and intimidation
two senior losers
establish the script
their desire to kill
transformed, disguised:
an overtly political act
in the name of all oppressed
kids victimized by peers.

You used to call me a fag.
Who's the fag now?

After the website
with the hit list
the gun list
the handmade explosives
the videos and rants
threats and arrests
visits to psychiatrists
medication and counseling

they spent a year
making the terror plan.

Peek-a-boo.
We know you're in there.

The terror plot:
become famous
FAMOUS
infamous
antiheroes
social media sensations

role models
cool
martyrs
to an unjust system:
high school.

The plot fails
and is wildly successful.

Who's ready to die next?

On April 20, 1999, two seniors executed a terrorist attack on their high school in Columbine, Colorado. They planted multiple explosive devices in an attempt to blow up the school, then shoot the evacuating survivors. When most of the devices failed, they methodically covered the school grounds, shooting people at close range, killing 13 and injuring 21 before killing themselves. A significant number of school shooters have been influenced by the Columbine massacre, and numerous copycat shootings have occurred since.

Hatfields & McCoys

The kid had a reason—
maybe he did
maybe he didn't—
to shoot a man—
maybe he did
maybe he didn't—
leave him
dead
in the street.

The people in the neighborhoods
don't want us here.

Payback came in
through gaps
in the school fence
morning gym class
kids in shorts, running
laughing, flirting
young in the sweet spring air.

Payback had an AK47
a semi-automatic pistol
aimed and fired
multiple times
at the kid—
who maybe did
or didn't
kill someone else.

They don't speak our language.

Three girls shot
others injured
in the stampede,
the kid on the ground
dead at 15.

Police asked everyone
at the school
what they saw—
maybe they did
maybe they didn't—
kids shook their heads
shrugged, looked away.

They won't talk to us.

Payback never sleeps
and the kid's friends—
maybe they did
maybe they didn't—
took their weapons
shot some relatives
close friends
of the school
shooters
dead
in the street.

This went on
and is going on still.

*On April 14, 2003, 2 men entered the campus and shot a 15-year-old
student during gym class at John McDonogh High School in New
Orleans. He died on the scene, and 3 other students were wounded*

while others were injured trying to escape the gunfire. None of the estimated 150 witnesses would provide information to investigators. Eventually, the perpetrators were caught and incarcerated. But revenge was taken on behalf of the victim, with relatives and friends of the shooters also shot and killed.

Red Lake

Sage burns for the man
who lays siege to himself
his two-day standoff
with his own father—
a tribal police officer—
ends with a gun
to his own sorry mouth
dirt's greedy teeth
in the flesh of his rot.

Burning sage fills the air
eight years later
the big son in black
trench coat, eyeliner
shoots his grandfather—
police officer and caretaker—
trigger finger in the DNA
destiny in the cold dry ground.

The smell of sage fills his head
as he dons his grand-
father's bullet-
proof vest,
takes the old man's guns
drives the old man's cruiser
through the rez
to the high school.

Sage, sage, fucking sage
kills the security officer
shoots a teacher, students
metal wrecked bodies

pile up, up, up
before his
hits the floor—

Game Over.

*On March 21, 2005, a troubled 16-year-old Native American boy
who lived in Red Lake, Minnesota, went on 2 killing sprees on the
Ojibwa reservation. He killed his grandfather, then took his vest,
weapons, and police vehicle to the high school, where he killed 7
people and wounded 5. After a shootout with the police, he killed
himself in an empty classroom. His father had committed suicide in a
similar manner following a 2-day standoff with the Red Lake Police.*

New Hope

Fall light tumbles fast
across rich green grass
fat trees fading
to gold and burnt umber
full uddered cows
grazing by red barns.

Live separately from the world's sins.

The milk truck driver
stops by the Amish
one-room schoolhouse,
asks the teacher, her students
about a clevis pin.

Salvation is not guaranteed.

He holds a handgun
on the boys
as they unload
his pickup
he boards up
the door.

You must show your faith by how you live.

The boys are released
a pregnant woman
parents with infants.
The girls must stay.

Always be modest, reserved, quiet.

At home he's scrawled
four notes
for his wife and children
who don't understand
will never understand.

Submit, obey, be humble.

Lined up at the chalkboard
waiting to answer a question
recite a poem, a prayer
die by a stranger's hand
the girls beg for death
first, to spare the others.

Blood and flesh
blood and bone
spatter the classroom.

Salvation is not guaranteed.

Six months later
New Hope School
opens its doors
to all who pass by.

*On October 2, 2006, a truck driver stopped at West Nickel Mines, a
one-room schoolhouse in Amish country in Lancaster County,
Pennsylvania. When he brandished a gun, the teacher ran for help.
After boarding up the door, the driver held as hostages 10 girls ages
6 to 13. The police tried to negotiate but he shot 8 of the girls, then
killed himself. After the massacre, the Amish people spoke of the
need for forgiveness, offering comfort to the killer's widow and
family.*

The Question Mark Kid

I would not speak
my name and you
forced me into this corner.

The door is chained
the guns are loaded
the video has been sent
so all will know.

Look at my mouth
it whispers to you.
Come closer.
Go away.

Teach me how to speak
how to share
where to go.

I am not from here
you just loved to crucify
me, inducing cancer
in my small shorn head.

I am in North Carolina
vacationing with Vladimir Putin.

I am the savior of the oppressed,
the poor and neglected.

Hollow-point bullets
expand in soft tissue
doing more damage

than full metal jackets.
I have more than 400
here for you.

Thanks to you, I will die
like Jesus Christ
inspire generations of weak
and defenseless people.

A name, I know not
how to tell who I am.

I write for the masses
sick of rich hedonists
the depraved who treat us
like dog shit.

Read my plays, hear
my unspoken poems
watch me rampage
through the halls
of Virginia Tech.

On April 16, 2007, an English major at Virginia Polytechnic Institute and State University shot a student in a dorm room, then killed the resident assistant who came to help. After mailing a video manifesto and writings to NBC News, the killer chained the front doors of the Engineering Science and Mechanics building. He fired more than 170 rounds at faculty and students. An engineering professor and Holocaust survivor held the door to his lecture hall closed so students could escape through the windows; he was shot multiple times and was awarded the Order of the Star of Romania posthumously for his bravery. The death toll included 4 other teachers and 27 students, with 17 wounded. The shooter killed himself when police arrived. He had selective mutism, and wrote such violent poetry and plays in a creative writing course the professor had him removed from the class.

Forward Together Forward

Forward in oceanography class
in the big lecture hall
smooth creatures slide
through clear blue water
their colors shimmering
their fins slapping to
the musical heartbeat
of a killer whale.

The fish are in schools.

Together by the stage
row upon row of students
the lecture down front
where a door is kicked open
he comes in wearing
a tee-shirt that says *Terrorist*
on an assault weapon design.

He's not kidding.

Forward the shotgun
out of the guitar case
he shoots to kill, kill, kill…

The wave surges back
to freedom from death
he takes out the pistol
loaded magazines
he struts the aisle
shooting fish in a barrel.

What's left behind
quivers and reverberates.

Together the kids shout
he's reloading
swim for their lives
before he shoots them,
shoots himself.

Forward the building
remodeled
a memorial garden
trees and benches
serenity
five red granite walls
each dead student's name
the silver sculpture lures
like a bait hook:
Remembered.

*On February 14, 2008, a former grad student entered Cole Hall at
Northern Illinois University in Dekalb. He wore a utility belt with
loaded magazines and several handguns, and he carried a guitar
case with a 12-gauge shotgun. Entering the auditorium near the
stage, he shot at students as he walked the aisles, killing himself
before the police arrived. Five students died, 17 were wounded, and
4 others injured trying to escape. The phrase "forward together"
comes from the school song.*

This is Not a Whodunit

In the novel, the protagonist is a biologist at a university trying to track down the source of a global pandemic. A Harvard PhD, she's suicidal because she might lose tenure—even though the rest of the world is facing obliteration.

In the real life version, the biologist loses tenure when her students complain and the committee sees her behavior as erratic, crazy.

In the novel, the young protagonist shoots her friend's brother by mistake while trying to scare her friend. In the real life version, the biologist shoots her younger brother, then runs to a used car lot brandishing the gun. In the newspaper version, actor Patrick Duffy's parents were killed by someone who did this. In the real life version, a newspaper clipping about Duffy's parents is in the protagonist's bedroom on the day she kills her brother.

In the novel, the protagonist spreads a fatal virus by creating a viral bomb. In the real life version, the biology department is afraid she might have actually done this with herpes, the focus of her post-doctoral work.

In the real life version, the woman stands up at a faculty meeting and begins to execute her peers, shooting them in the head one by one. When the handgun jams, the survivors rush her, shoving her out of the room.

In the movie version, the protagonist punches another mother in the head when the woman takes the last booster seat at IHOP.

In the video game, the killer sends letter bombs to her old boss after he questions her research skills.

In the prison version, the protagonist tells her writing group her novels are her ticket out.

In the tragic version, the protagonist says, "It didn't happen. There's no way. They're still alive."

And she believes it.

On February 12, 2010, a biology professor at University of Alabama, Huntsville, stood up at a routine faculty meeting and began shooting her peers. Denied tenure, she was in her final semester at the school. She killed 3 and wounded 3 before her gun malfunctioned. Research into her past unearthed previous violent acts including shooting and killing her brother, an act which was ruled accidental at the time. Her unpublished novels cover themes that echo her own life story.

The Unique Divine Inspiration

We believe in the Bible
given for the faith of the believing
in the return of tuition payments
if a student is expelled.

We believe in the Bible,
it is infallibly and uniquely
authoritative and free
from any errors
at the business park
near the airport
planes roaring overhead
during classes, hands folded
eyes on the searing blue sky.

We believe in the Bible
full historicity and perspicuity
of its record of primeval history
including the literal existence
of Adam and Eve and Satan
and handguns in a nursing class
lining up students
against the wall:
"I am going to kill you all!"

We believe in the Bible
in the resurrection of the body
the final judgment
the eternal felicity of the righteous
fleeing down the hall
shooting random targets
hijacking a dead student's car.

We believe in the Bible
the fulfillment of His purposes
in the works of creation
and redemption
with eternal rewards
and punishments
parking at the Safeway
wandering fluorescent aisles
wondering about God
and His bible and all that.

On April 2, 2012, a former student attended a nursing class at Oikos University, a Korean Christian college in Oakland, California. He shot and killed 7 fellow students and injured 3, then drove a stolen car to a nearby supermarket, where he was apprehended. Deemed mentally incompetent to stand trial, he was eventually sentenced to 7 consecutive life sentences.

Dance Dance Revolution

Look at me.

He liked to go to the movie theater
and play the dance step game
or World of Warcraft
in his dark bedroom
in his mother's house
in the basement
black garbage bags
over all the windows.

Look at me.

Diagnoses and therapy
medications, special ed
homeschool, homebound
isolation, frustration
a house full of guns
a room full of guns
a tomb full of guns.

Look at me.

Gun safe, 1400
rounds of ammunition
6 firearms, a vest
5 miles to the school
for kindergarten through fourth.

*Help me! I don't want
to be here!*

In 5 minutes
156 shots
at first graders
curled into balls.

Look at them.

Parents and teachers
testifying to legislators
suing gun manufacturers
protests and lectures
marches and interviews
those left behind
in their not so quiet grief.

Look at them.

Same dance, same steps
over and over
faster and faster
more and more tragic.
Some states pass
the assault weapons ban.
Congress refuses.

*Mommy, I'm okay
but all my friends are dead.*

*On December 14, 2012, a disturbed 20-year-old killed his mother.
He brought some of her cache of arms and ammunition to Sandy
Hook Elementary School in Newtown, Connecticut, where he
murdered 20 6- and 7-year old children and 6 staff with a military
grade weapon. After the tragedy, global protest and near universal
support for the banning of assault weapons in the US was met with*

43

13 Minutes

*Dear sir we regret to inform
you are ineligible
to purchase a firearm
in the state of California.*

So you build an AR-15
from parts you buy
legally
and a tactical
vest, black
clothing with pockets
for the ammo you carry
40 magazines
with 30 rounds
to your dad's house.

You are not ineligible
to light a fire and you set one
shoot your brother
shoot your dad
mother
out of town.

Out in the street you
carjack a stranger
make her drive you
to the college
you dropped out of
shoot the woman
who intercedes
shoot the bus
that passes by

shoot the SUV
the campus groundskeeper
his young daughter.

You are ineligible to enter
the college library
you shoot the old woman
collecting cans, open fire
on students
on library staff.

In your bedroom
a letter from California
Department of Justice:
Dear sir we regret to inform
you are ineligible
to purchase a firearm
in the state of California.

*A 23-year-old man went on a 13-minute killing spree in Santa
Monica on June 7, 2013, after setting fire to his father's house and
shooting to death his brother and father. He carjacked a vehicle and
shot bystanders on the way to Santa Monica College, where he
opened fire on students and faculty in the library. Since President
Obama was in town for a fundraiser, specialized tactical resources
were in the area and responded rapidly, killing the shooter.
Ineligible to purchase a gun due to a history of violent threats and
bomb making activities, he built one himself.*

The Sane One

Look at that woman
she's hot. She doesn't see
you or know your name.

Look at that guy
he's a veteran
doesn't know you
doesn't want to.

Other people think I'm crazy
but I'm not.
I'm the sane one.

Look at your home
the 14 guns
the trips to shooting ranges
with your mom.

Look at your academic record
flunking out
time to take a stand
for what you stand for.

A man who was known
by no one
is now known
by everyone.

Look at the hot girls
jump when you speak
respond when you approach

in your flak jacket
handgun in their faces.

Look at the veteran flail
at your feet, bleeding
begging
after helping students
escape their due.

*His face splashed across
every screen, his name
across the lips
of every person
on the planet.*

Look at the plainclothes detectives
lined up in the hall
just like on TV
shoot them
before you shoot yourself.

*On October 1, 2015, a 26-year-old student at Umpqua Community
College near Roseburg, Oregon, fatally shot the assistant professor
and 8 students in his writing class, wounding 8 others. He handed a
package of his writings about infamy and violent acts to one student
to give to the police. The shooter killed himself after being wounded
in a brief shootout. He had 6 weapons with him, and police found 8
more at his home, all legally purchased. An Army veteran who
ushered students from the connecting classroom, alerted students in
another building, and returned to try to help more students was shot
5 times but survived.*

Future Mass Shooter

drops out of high school
works at a gas station
lives at home
trolls alt-right sites
roots for Trump
praises Hitler
asks where to find
cheap assault rifles
to kill a lot of people.

Work sucks, school sucks, life sucks.

The future mass shooter
jokes about Columbine
jokes about Sandy Hook
buys a semi-automatic
mingles with the students
at his old high school.

8:00 a.m. die.

The future mass shooter
gears up in the boys room
shoots a football player
shoots a cheerleader
shoots up the computer lab
shoots up and down the hall
shooting, reloading, shooting
reloading, shooting, reloading
shooting himself.

I just want out of this shit.

On December 7, 2017, a 21-year-old dropout from Aztec High School in Aztec, New Mexico, trespassed on school property with a loaded handgun. He shot 2 students and tried to kill more before committing suicide. The previous year he had been investigated by the FBI after posting on an online forum about buying weapons for a mass shooting. He did not own a firearm at the time, but bought one legally a month before the shooting.

Hurt in 42

He oversleeps,
Mom drives him
drops him off
a kiss for a good day
at school.

Don't Panic.

Band room's packed
with friends, all safe.

In the common area
his experiment begins:
he will shoot to kill.
How will students respond?
How will the school react?
The public, the world?

So long and thanks for all the fish.

He's interested
in science, reads
fiction, plays
the trombone.
He's 15, kills 2
wounds 14 more.

*This gun has a right end
and a wrong end.*

He wanted to break
the monotony.

He stole it
from his parents' bedroom.
He hid it
in a basket of laundry
his book bag
his plan.

*A gun for going out
and making people miserable with.*

His life had no purpose
nobody's does. All
of this:
an experiment.

He looked for an answer
to the ultimate question
of life, the universe

and everything.

*He hoped and prayed
there wasn't an afterlife.*

*On January 23, 2018, a Marshall County High School student in
Benton, Kentucky, opened fire on classmates, killing 2 and wounding
14. He told investigators it was an experiment. In his bedroom they
found books and other materials related to weaponry, violence, and
the military. An online post referred to the popular novel* The
Hitchhiker's Guide to the Galaxy *and stated, "Sorry for the kids that
I may hurt in 42."*

School Strong

Another day in paradise
blue sky cloudless
spring in the air
valentines in their hearts
and then it begins…

another senseless rampage
a boy with soldiers' weapons
hate in his heart
shooting from above.
Children scatter
in the courtyard below:

17 dead
17 wounded

all those who survive
their lives
forever changed
millions watching
the horror unfold.

We
are
going
to be
the last
mass
shooting!

And the governor
signs a bill

and secures more guns in schools…

We
call
BS!

And the school orders see-through
backpacks and more screenings
and the legislators say to pray
and continue to do nothing…

We
call
BS!

At the school
at other schools
in the streets
in the parks
everywhere
around the country
students protest
and register to vote
against the gun legislators
and the gun lobbyists
and the gun manufacturers
and the gun retailers
against the killing fields
in US schools.

Around the world
the people rally
millions gather
brave young voices
fill the spring air:

Do something!

On February 14, 2018, a 19-year-old student expelled from Marjory Stoneman Douglas High School in Parkland, Florida, arrived on campus with guns and ammunition. He killed 17 people and wounded 17 more before escaping with the evacuating students. He was identified and arrested soon after. Local law enforcement had received multiple calls about the disturbed young man's constant threats to commit the very act he carried out, yet he was able to legally purchase firearms. Surviving students organized protests, walkouts, marches, and demonstrations demanding gun control and getting out the vote against legislators who receive political contributions from gun lobbies. Note: quotes are from Emma González, a student leader from the school.

Post-Parkland

At sunrise you leave
your sleeping family
weapon under one arm
or tucked in a leather satchel
drive slow to work.

Open carry
stand your ground
safety first.

A regulated violence
invades the suburban hush
haunting memories
the surge and pelt
of bullets in the brain
pan, the long bone.
Each time you review
the sky gets darker.

Hours of training
local permits
safety first.

You park in the lot
beside the muscle cars
parental Mercedes
shitbox American-mades
head for the building
the weight of the .32
like a hug from a friend.

New Florida Law: conceal
the weapon
target practice
safety first.

You teach
the children, protect
the innocent now
pockmarked
with terror holes
the future a long barrel
with no light at the end.

There's a name for what
you do for your students:
No Guns
Left Behind.

Appendix: In Memoriam

The following list includes the names and ages of the 177 innocent people who died from gunshot wounds acquired during the school shootings described in the poems you just read. The list of victims of gunshot wounds received while on campuses or in other locations such as neighborhood streets, movie theaters, cars, parks, airports, and their own homes, is, of course, much longer. Much, much longer—and growing.

There have been more school shootings since the one in Parkland, Florida.

Enoch Brown, teacher
9 students (names and ages unknown)

University of Texas, Austin:
Martin (Mark) Gabour, 16
Thomas Frederick Eckman, 18
Thomas Aquinas Ashton, 22
Karen Griffith, 17
Thomas Ray Karr, 24
David Hubert Gunby, 23
Claudia Rutt, 18
Paul Bolton Sonntag, 18
Roy Dell Schmidt, 29
Billy Paul Speed, 24
Robert Hamilton Boyer, 33
Harry Walchuk, 38
Marguerite Lamport, 45
Edna Elizabeth Townsley, 51
Baby Boy Wilson, unborn

Kent State:
Sandra Lee Scheuer, 20
Jeffrey Gleennn Miller, 20
Alison B. Krause, 19
William Knox Schroeder, 19

Cal State, Fullerton:
Deborah Paulsen
Donald E. Karges
Seth Fessenden
Bruce A, Jacobson
Paul Herzberg
Stephen Becker
Frank Teplansky

Cleveland Elementary:
Burton Wragg, 52
Mike Suchar, 56

Jonesboro, Arkansas:
Natalie Brooks, 11
Paige Ann Herring, 12
Stephanie Johnson, 12
Brittney Ryen Varner, 11
Shannon Wright, 32

Thurston High School:
Ben Walker, 17
Mikael Nickolauson, 17

Columbine:
Rachel Scott, 17
Daniel Rohrbough, 15
Kyle Velasquez, 16

Steven Curnow, 14
Cassie Bernall, 17
Isaiah Shoels, 18
Matthew Kechter, 16
Lauren Townsend, 18
John Tomlin, 16
Kelly Fleming, 16
Daniel Mauser, 15
Corey DePooter, 17
William David Sanders, 47

John McDonogh High School:
Jonathan Williams, 15

Red Lake:
Alicia Alberta White, 14
Thurlene Marie Stillday, 15
Chanelle Star Rosebear, 15
Chase Albert Lussier, 15
Dewayne Michael Lewis, 15
Derrick Brian Brun, 28
Neva Jane Wynkoop-Rogers, 62

West Nickel Mines:
Naomi Rose Ebersol, 7
Marian Stoltzfus Fisher, 13
Anna Mae Stoltzfus, 12
Lena Zook Miller, 8
Mary Liz Miller, 7

Virginia Tech:
Ross Alameddine, 20
Brian Bluhm, 25
Ryan Clark, 22

Austin Cloyd, 18
Daniel Perez Cueva, 21
Matthew Gwaltney, 24
Caitlin Hammaren, 19
Jeremy Herbstritt, 27
Rachael Hill, 18
Emily Hilscher, 19
Matthew La Porte, 20
Jarrett Lane, 22
Henry Lee, 20
Lauren McCain, 20
Daniel O'Neil, 22
Juan Ortiz, 26
Minal Panchal, 26
Erin Peterson, 18
Michael Pohle Jr., 23
Julia Pryde, 23
Mary Karen Read, 19
Reema Samaha, 18
Leslie Sherman, 20
Maxine Turner, 22
Nicole White, 20
Waleed Shaalan, 32
Partahi Lumbantoruan, 34
Jamie Bishop, 35
Jocelyne Couture-Nowak, 49
Kevin Granata, 45
Liviu Librescu, 76
G. V. Loganathan, 53

Northern Illinois University:
Catalina Garcia, 20
Ryanne Mace, 19
Gayle Dubowski, 20

Daniel Parmenter, 20
Julianna Gehant, 32

University of Alabama, Huntsville:
Gopi Podila, 52
Maria Ragland Davis, 50
Adriel D. Johnson, 53

Oikos University:
Lydia Sim, 21
Grace Eunhae Kim, 23
Katleen Ping, 24
Tshering Rinzing Bhutia, 38
Doris Chibuko, 40
Sonam Chodon, 33
Judith Seymour, 53

Sandy Hook Elementary School:
Charlotte Bacon, 6
Daniel Barden, 7
Olivia Engel, 6
Josephine Gay, 7
Dylan Hockley, 6
Madeleine Hsu, 6
Catherine Hubbard, 6
Chase Kowalski, 7
Jesse Lewis, 6
Ana Márquez-Greene, 6
James Mattioli, 6
Grace McDonnell, 7
Emilie Parker, 6
Jack Pinto, 6
Noah Pozner, 6
Caroline Previdi, 6
Jessica Rekos, 6

Avielle Richman, 6
Benjamin Wheeler, 6
Allison Wyatt, 6
Rachel D'Avino, 29
Dawn Hochsprung, 47
Anne Marie Murphy, 52
Lauren Rousseau, 30
Mary Sherlach, 56
Victoria Leigh Soto, 27

Santa Monica College:
Marcela Dia Franco, 26
Carlos Navarro Franco, 68
Margarita Gomez, 68

Umpqua Community College:
Lucero Alcaraz, 19
Treven Taylor Anspach, 20
Rebecka Ann Carnes, 18
Quinn Glen Cooper, 18
Lucas Eibel, 18
Kim Saltmarsh Dietz, 59
Jason Dale Johnson, 33
Lawrence Levine, 67
Sarena Dawn Moore, 44

Aztec High School:
Casey Jordan Marquez, 17
Francisco Fenandez, 18

Marshall County High School:
Bailey Nicole Holt, 15
Preston Ryan Cope, 15

Marjory Stoneman Douglas High School:
Alyssa Alhadeff, 14
Martin Duque, 14
Nicholas Dworet, 17
Jaime Guttenberg, 14
Luke Hoyer, 15
Cara Loughran, 14
Gina Montalto, 14
Joaquin Oliver, 17
Alaina Petty, 14
Meadow Pollack, 18
Helena Ramsay, 17
Alex Schachter, 14
Carmen Schentrup, 16
Peter Wang, 15
Scott Beigel, 35
Aaron Feis, 37
Chris Hixon, 49

www.ingramcontent.com/pod-product-compliance
Lightning Source LLC
LaVergne TN
LVHW041118180726
843490LV00003B/1070